"This is another good elaboration or an aspect of IFS. It contains helpful categories and guidelines as well as a powerful transcript of a session."

— Richard Schwartz, PhD, creator of the IFS Model, author of *Internal Family Systems Therapy* and *You are the One You've Been Waiting For*

"Working with the emotions and behaviors of clients' anger can be challenging for therapists. Will containment or expression of the anger be more helpful? This clear and thorough booklet considers these questions relative to various parts that hold burdens of anger and offers the IFS therapist specific help with this complex topic."

— Susan McConnell, Senior Lead Trainer for the Center for Self Leadership

"In this booklet, Jay Earley examines and differentiates the roles and purpose anger plays in our internal world. Jay carefully dissects the many forms of anger and how to deal with them effectively and respectfully. He brings clarity to the issue of when anger needs to be expressed internally or externalized in the therapy session or in the client's external world. A thoughtful guide to fully understanding anger and how to work with it in order to strengthen and heal clients' internal worlds and external relationships. A wonderful addition to the IFS professional literature."

— Marla Silverman, Ph.D., IFS Therapist, Couples Therapy Trainer, Gestalt Center for Psychotherapy and Training Faculty

Books and Booklets
by Jay Earley, PhD

The IFS Series
Self-Therapy
Self-Therapy for Your Inner Critic (with Bonnie Weiss)
Resolving Inner Conflict

The IFS Professional Booklet Series
Working with Anger in IFS
Negotiating for Self-Leadership*

The Pattern System^{SM} Series
Embracing Intimacy
Working Through Procrastination
and Achieving Your Goals*

The Inner Critic Series (with Bonnie Weiss)
Activating Your Inner Champion
Instead of Your Inner Critic
Letting Go of Perfectionism*

Interactive Group Therapy

Transforming Human Culture

Inner Journeys

*Forthcoming

Working with Anger

in Internal Family Systems Therapy

Jay Earley, PhD

■ PATTERN SYSTEM BOOKS

Larkspur, CA

Pattern System Books
140 Marina Vista Ave.
Larkspur, CA 94939
415-924-5256
www.patternsystembooks.com

ISBN: 978-0-9843927-8-0
ISBN-10: 0-9843927-8-5
LCCN: 2012935419

Printed in the United States of America

Contents

Acknowledgments

I am very grateful to Richard Schwartz, PhD, for creating the amazing IFS Model, which has completely transformed not only the way I do therapy but also my creative life of theorizing and writing. Susan McConnell provided detailed, intelligent feedback that helped me to greatly improve this booklet. I also received valuable feedback from Bonnie Weiss and Marla Silverman.

Jeannene Langford continued her excellent work with my book covers, and Kira Freed continued her fine work of editing and proofreading. Larry Kaye did a great job of converting to ebook format.

Introduction to the
IFS Professional Booklet Series

This is one of a series of booklets that cover advanced topics in IFS theory and practice. Some of the booklets describe concepts that are well known in the professional IFS community but that haven't been put into written form before. Other booklets introduce original ideas about how to practice IFS more effectively or understand its theory in a fuller way.

In my opinion, IFS is by far the most effective and respectful psychotherapy model. At this point, it is taught mostly through an excellent professional training program rather than through writings. Therefore, the professional literature on IFS hasn't yet done justice to the profound nature of the approach. This series, along with my other IFS books, attempts to remedy this situation.

Introduction

This booklet is intended primarily for Internal Family Systems Therapy (IFS) therapists and practitioners. It assumes a knowledge of the IFS view of the psyche and the IFS method. It should also be useful to therapists not trained in IFS or who are new to the IFS Model, so I have included a glossary in which the basic IFS concepts are defined.

Internal Family Systems Therapy (IFS) is a cutting-edge psychotherapy approach that has been spreading rapidly around the country and the world over the last decade. It is the signature work of pioneering psychologist Richard Schwartz. IFS is extremely powerful for accessing deep psychological wounds and healing them. It is especially effective with trauma, and there has been increasing interest in IFS among trauma specialists. IFS is also quite effective at helping clients with everyday life issues and with spiritual development.

Schwartz, originally a family systems therapist, started working with his clients' inner worlds and discovered their subpersonalities, which he calls *parts*. He realized that his clients' parts were related to each other in systems that were similar to those he recognized in families, hence the name "Internal Family Systems Therapy."[1] IFS is user friendly. It

---

1. For more information on IFS, read *The Internal Family Systems Model* by Richard Schwartz, Guilford Press, 1995, and visit the Center for Self Leadership at www.selfleadership.org.

is easy for clients to understand its concepts and natural for most of them to access and relate to their parts.

Anger is an emotion that is problematic for many people. With other emotions, the main question is usually whether or not to feel or show the emotion. With anger, the situation is often more complicated because anger can be harmful and destructive when acted out. Therefore, many of us have conflicting attitudes about anger. We live in a violent society, surrounded by examples of the destructive effects of anger, and some of us have been victims of it. Anger and violence are sometimes also celebrated—in war, gangs, sports, and criminal TV shows. Working with anger in therapy is therefore tricky and complex.

Anger can arise in various ways in Internal Family Systems Therapy, depending on which part holds the anger, what function the anger serves, and whether the anger is disowned. Each situation requires a different type of therapeutic intervention. Protector anger that is being acted out needs to be understood so you can heal the exile being protected. Expressing such anger is usually not a good idea. Exile anger, on the other hand, needs to be welcomed and expressed in sessions in order to fully witness the exile and also as a way of helping the exile to feel protected and safe from harm. Disowned anger also needs to be expressed in sessions as a way of accessing and developing the client's strength and healthy aggression.

When anger comes up in a session, it is helpful to understand the context and dynamics you are facing so you know how to proceed. This booklet discusses various approaches to working with anger as part of the IFS process and the circumstances in which each can be used most effectively.

CHAPTER 1

Protective Anger

Protector Anger

The most common form of anger we see in IFS sessions is the anger of a *protector*—a manager or firefighter—that is using it to defend against the pain of an exile. The protector uses anger as a way to avoid feeling the pain that the exile is holding. Because of this, the anger often arises in situations in which it is inappropriate and is frequently more extreme than is warranted.

For example, when James feels rejected by a woman he has been dating, he often feels very angry at her. He doesn't express the anger to her, but it can become pretty intense inside. This anger is an attempt to protect him from feeling the pain of an exile who feels hurt and unlovable. It distracts him from those vulnerable emotions and substitutes a more acceptable feeling.

Protector anger may also be an attempt to protect an exile from a perceived external threat. For example, let's look at the case of one client, Marlene. Whenever someone acts controlling or dominant toward Marlene, or when she perceives their behavior in this way, a protector is activated that feels angry at the person.

Marlene often expresses her anger at the person she feels controlled by. She tries to prove to the person that he or she is wrong for trying to control her. This is an attempt to protect the exile from being dominated. Because Marlene's anger is protector-driven, it tends to be either inappropriate or too intense a response to what the other person has actually done. As a result, it often offends people or makes them worry that Marlene will get out of control They often respond with increased attempts to control her, resulting in exactly what her Angry Part fears.

There are four situations involving protector anger, each requiring a somewhat different strategy:

1. The anger is being acted out in the client's life.
2. The anger is felt, but the Self refrains from acting it out.
3. The anger is felt, but protectors prevent it from being acted out.
4. The anger is disowned.

We will explore each of them separately.

Protective Anger Being Acted Out

For protector anger that is being acted out, the protocol for IFS work is straightforward. The client accesses the *Self*, gets to know the angry protector, and develops a trusting relationship with this part. Then the Self gets permission to work with the *exile* being protected, witnesses the origins of this experience, and goes through the steps to unburden this exile. Then the protector can let go of its anger because there is no longer a need to protect this exile.

Marlene worked with her Angry Part and developed some appreciation of why it felt such an intense need to protect her. Then she accessed an exile who had been rigidly controlled by her parents. She witnessed this childhood situation and the exile's feelings of being cornered and power-less, and then in her imagination she retrieved the part from that situation into one in which it had the freedom it craved. Then it was ready to go through an unburdening process to release its feelings of domination and powerlessness. Once this part was unburdened, Marlene's Angry Part could let go of its need to protect her.

When anger is being acted out, it is often helpful to do additional work with the client on learning to contain it and interact appropriately. First the client needs to get to know the angry part and develop a trusting relationship with it so that the Self can help the part to refrain from acting out.

As an illustration of working with this type of anger, Marlene had a tendency to flip out at work and yell at her boss. After working on this issue for a while, Marlene got to know her Angry Part and understood that it was trying to protect her from being dominated. Even though it was creating problems, Marlene appreciated its attempts to protect her. This helped the part to trust her.

Marlene made an agreement with her Angry Part that when Marlene got angry at work, her Self could intervene and take a time-out to cool down before Marlene's Angry Part yelled at anyone. This Self-leadership kept her from getting into trouble and actually reduced the reactions from her boss that were upsetting this part.

Constructive Communication of Anger

In this type of situation, it can be helpful to teach a client communication skills that involve *speaking for* an angry part rather than *speaking from* it. The client learns to speak for a part by making statements such as, "A part of me got angry when you said that." When a client is speaking **for** a part, the client is in Self, as opposed to speaking **from** the part, in which case the client is *blended* with the part and is acting out its feelings. A client who is completely identified with an angry part might say things such as, "You are such a controlling bastard."

When clients speak **for** angry parts, they aren't likely to trigger other people to become angry at them in return. Clients can also communicate what is making them angry in a way that maximizes the chances that they will be heard and therefore get what they want.

It may be helpful to have the client practice this kind of communication in a therapy session by role-playing a life situation that involves anger.[2] This is good practice for communicating anger constructively in real life.

Ultimately, you want to work with this kind of anger in the regular IFS way for it to be unburdened, but establishing this kind of Self-leadership may be necessary first. With Marlene, after she made the agreement that stopped the acting out, her Angry Part was able to calm down because there was more peace in the office.

In addition, by speaking **for** her Angry Part, Marlene reassured the part that she was now strong enough to speak up for her needs, so she would be less likely to be dominated as in the past. Therefore the Angry Part would feel less of a need to take over. Then in her IFS therapy, it was easier to get permission from the Angry Part to access the

---

2. Marshall Rosenberg has developed an excellent method for communicating in conflictual situations called *Nonviolent Communication.* PuddleDancer Press, 2003.

exile it was protecting and go through the healing process described above.

In some cases, it can be helpful to unburden some of the anger before continuing with the rest of the process. This is often the case when the anger is intense, bitter, raging, or revengeful. In these cases, the protector will feel a need for the unburdening.

Unburdening a protector usually happens at the very end of the whole IFS sequence, after the exile has been unburdened, but in this case, it can be helpful to unburden some of the anger that the protector is carrying before even working with the exile. This helps to calm things down internally because the parts of the client that are polarized with the angry part will also become less intense. For example, if Marlene had a part that shamed her for losing control of her anger at work, this part would be able to relax.

The procedure for unburdening anger is similar to what is used with an exile. You have the client sense where the anger is carried in the protector's body, and then the protector releases some of the anger to one of the elements—light, water, wind, earth, or fire.

Unburdening some of the anger also helps the client to be less provocative in interactions with people. And since the client won't be provoking other people's anger so much, the client's angry part won't get triggered so often. This can make the rest of the IFS process easier.

Protective Rage Being Suppressed

Let's look at two situations in which rage is suppressed and the enraged part is vilified.

Rage Felt but Suppressed

Sometimes a protector has anger, or even rage, that is felt by the client but suppressed by other protectors and therefore isn't acted out. Rage is usually suppressed because of the danger of its being expressed destructively. Sometimes there really **is** a danger of a harmful expression of rage. In other cases, the client wouldn't really act it out; however, a protector may be afraid of it because anger was punished in the client's family of origin.

Even though this anger isn't being acted out explicitly, it will often leak out in subtle ways that poison the client's relationships, and sometimes the client may explode in rage (see below).

Suppression is common with firefighter rage. It often carries tremendous charge, which frightens other parts. This tends to cause a major polarization in the system because managers arise to try to stop it from being acted out, and they create conflict with the enraged firefighter. These managers very often vilify the rageful part. If the client sees an image of the part, it often looks nasty and evil.

For example, one of my clients would get enraged at people whom he perceived as not respecting him, but he didn't express it to them. This rage was experienced by an angry firefighter but suppressed by a manager that realized it could get him into trouble. So it ate away at him inside.

Suppressing anger is fundamentally different from **refraining from expressing** anger. Suppression comes from managers that try to exile the angry part and often criticize or shame it. Refraining comes from the Self, which chooses not to express anger because it wouldn't be helpful. The Self makes no judgment about the anger. The person accepts his or her anger and may even appreciate the reason for feeling it, but doesn't act on it.

Occasional Outbursts of Rage

Another common situation involves a client suppressing his or her rage most of the time and perhaps not even feeling it, but occasionally he or she explodes in rage or loses control in an angry outburst. These explosions usually scare the client as well as whoever is the target of the anger.

For example, Don didn't have a big issue with anger most of the time, but every once in a while, his wife would do something that triggered him to go on an angry rant at her. Whenever he did, she would be scared and deeply hurt. He would have no idea what had happened and would feel terrible about what he had done. He would vow to never do it again, but sooner or later it would recur.

When Don went inside to work on this part in an IFS session, he saw it as a huge, powerful demon. This image didn't represent what the part was actually like. Instead, it showed how much the part has been vilified in the view of Don's other parts. In other words, when Don was seeing the part this way, he wasn't in Self.

How to Work with These Situations

The following is a discussion of how to work with either of the above situations. Your goal is to get to know the enraged firefighter in a session. However, this may not be easy to do because access to this Enraged Part is often blocked by the suppressing manager. Therefore, you will have to get permission from the manager to work with the Enraged Part. Sometimes you can reassure the manager enough for it to give you permission, but sometimes you will have to work on the polarization between the Enraged Firefighter and manager in order to gain access.

To work with this polarization, first get to know the manager and obtain its permission to have a dialogue with the firefighter. Since the manager sees the Enraged Part as very dangerous and evil, you will need to help the client gain the manager's trust and provide reassurances of safety.

You and the client need to reassure the manager that you won't encourage the expression of the rage but rather that you're seeking to understand the Enraged Part's positive intent and what exile it is protecting. Explain that you (the therapist) will be there to make sure that nothing destructive happens.

Then when the two parts dialogue with each other, the client can help them to understand each other and lessen their internal battles. For more detailed information on how to work with polarization, see my book *Resolving Inner Conflict*. This polarization work may not completely resolve the conflict, but it should at least allow the client to get permission from the manager to work with the Enraged Part.

Once this has happened, the client can begin to get to know the Enraged Part and integrate it into his or her psyche. At this point, the rage loses its intensity, and the Enraged Part isn't so threatening. In fact, the image of the Enraged Part as powerful and evil often shifts to something much different. For example, once Don got to know his Enraged Part, it looked and felt like a towering column of presence.

This new view of the Enraged Part will often allow the polarization work to be completed or at least allow the client to make a good connection with it The client may even see the positive qualities it has to offer and welcome them into his or her psyche. For example, Don realized that what he had called his Enraged Part was actually a powerful sense of presence, which made him feel solid and potent. Welcoming positive qualities will be explained more in the next chapter.

The next step is for the client to get permission from the Enraged Part to work with the exile it is protecting and then to heal that part so the Enraged Part can relax. This was summarized above.

CHAPTER 2

Disowned Anger and Strength

Disowned Anger

In IFS, we sometimes encounter parts that have been disowned or exiled because their feelings or behavior are seen as unacceptable. Originally the part wasn't acceptable to the family of origin (or culture), and then it became unacceptable to other parts of the client as well, and this dynamic has carried forward into the present. In IFS, these parts are often called *protectors-in-exile* to distinguish them from exiles, which are disowned because of the pain they carry from childhood.

I will call these *disowned parts.* I am introducing this new term because the part that is exiled isn't always a protector. It can also be either an exile or a healthy or non-extreme part. Voice Dialogue[3] has a primary focus on this type of part, which it calls a "disowned self" as opposed to a "primary self."

Anger is probably the most common kind of disowned part. When clients have disowned their anger, they tend to lack assertiveness or strength. They may even be passive, pleasing, self-effacing, or lacking in self-confidence and drive. This is because their *strength* has become disowned

---

3. H. Stone & S. Winkleman, *Embracing Our Selves,* New World Library, 1989.

along with their anger.

This process is common among girls and women, although it is not confined to them. Because of both innate hormonal makeup and gender programming, the expression of anger tends to be fostered among males and discouraged among females. However, these are just cultural tendencies. Some men have disowned their anger, and some women act theirs out.

Let's look at an example. Donna's parents were judgmental and shaming whenever she got angry. They gave her the message that she was supposed to be a nice girl and not be aggressive or make waves. As a result, her anger got disowned, and this was enforced by managers that believed her anger was bad. Donna became meek and quiet and had a hard time asserting her needs or opinions.

Clients who have disowned their anger may occasionally have angry outbursts, due to the disowned angry part breaking through. This anger is usually extreme and inappropriate to the context. The person may feel ashamed of these incidents and believe that he or she has an anger problem. However, the real problem with the person's anger is that it is disowned.

Disowned anger can come from a protector, an exile, or even a healthy part. In the case in which it comes from an exile, the part is just responding in a naturally aggressive way to childhood insults or deprivations. However, this anger often becomes extreme **because** it is disowned. In other words, the part reacts to being disowned by becoming increasingly and irrationally angry.

In working with this type of anger, the goal is to gain access to the disowned angry part and welcome it back into the internal family of parts and into the client's conscious life, where it can live and express itself. It is helpful to do this even if the anger is extreme—though in this case, it should only be expressed in therapy sessions. Have the client witness the part's feelings, and encourage it to express the anger in whatever way it wants in a session. This is often a great relief to the client since the anger has been repressed for so long.

However, welcoming back the disowned anger may not be easy. There will probably be protectors that are frightened of it, and they will fight to keep it from being reowned. See the section below on how to deal with this.

Sometimes a disowned angry part will be carrying pain caused by the way the anger was not accepted in the client's family. For example, Donna's Angry Part could be carrying burdens of deficiency and shame because of the way her parents ridiculed her for her anger. In that case, the part is considered both a disowned part and an exile. It will need to go through the usual series of healing steps for an exile (witnessing, reparenting, retrieval, and unburdening) to complete its work.

In other cases, the pain from the disowning may be carried by a separate part, which is an exile. For example, Donna's Angry Part could only be carrying anger, and another part could be carrying the shame and sense of deficiency. In this case, Donna's Angry Part would only need to be welcomed back into her internal family and encouraged to express itself, and the process of exile healing would be done with the other part.

Strength

IFS recognizes that a protector-in-exile or disowned part often holds a positive quality or energy that can be integrated into the client's psyche. For example, sexuality, spontaneity, and caring are all positive qualities that could be disowned if they were unacceptable in the client's family of origin. When the disowned part is welcomed back, it allows the person to reown this positive energy.

When anger is disowned, it isn't the anger itself that is the positive quality to be reowned. There is a positive quality that gets disowned along with the anger, which I will call *strength*. Strength means healthy aggression, aliveness, personal power, and the ability to assert oneself. It includes the ability to take risks, adopt a powerful stance in the world, and feel a zest for life. In the Diamond Approach[4], this quality is called the Red Essence or Strength, and it is understood that when anger is blocked, the Red Essence is also blocked. Gestalt therapy[5] also recognizes healthy aggression as an important goal in therapy.

Anger is a natural protector reaction to injustice, boundary violations, mistreatment, or frustration of one's aims. When we are in Self, anger is rarely necessary because we can call on our healthy sense of power, forcefulness, and limit setting to handle these situations. We can be strong and assertive without frightening or harming other people. This is what I mean by healthy aggression or strength.

However, following the terminology of the Diamond Ap-

---

4. A. H. Almaas, *The Pearl Beyond Price*, p. 206-215, Diamond Books, 1988.
5. Perls, F., Hefferline, R. F., and Goodman, P. *Gestalt Therapy.* Bantam, 1951.

proach, I am using the term *strength* to include more than just healthy aggression and assertiveness. It also includes aliveness, expansiveness, passion, and being fully embodied. It is our life energy.

When we exile our anger, we also exile our strength, not because we intend to but because is the way the human psyche operates.

By welcoming back disowned anger, we open the possibility of reclaiming this positive quality of strength for ourselves. This is especially true if we welcome back the anger in an embodied way that includes feeling the anger fully and perhaps expressing it. This helps clients to embody their strength and aliveness.

When you facilitate a client in fully expressing his or her anger in a session, the focus is not on containing it or communicating it in a constructive way. It is on fully embodying the anger as a means of reowning the client's strength. This is **not** intended as practice for real-life interactions—it should only be done in a therapy session or when the client is alone. Practice for real-life communication of anger is an entirely different process, which was covered in Chapter 1.

Let's look at Donna's work: She first allowed herself to feel the emotion of anger that had been disowned. When this felt reasonably safe to the protectors who had disowned the anger, I encouraged her to notice how the anger manifested in her body in the moment. She noticed a clenching of her jaw, power in her arms, deeper breathing, and upright posture. At some point, she wanted to express the anger.

In subsequent sessions, I helped her to fully express her anger. One session involved hitting a pillow, another twisting a towel. These things allowed the anger to be fully embodied in a vibrant way. They encouraged her to feel the strength and aliveness that was awakened in her by owning and expressing her anger. She felt it as hot, streaming energy in her arms and a feeling of potency in her trunk.

What if the anger that has been disowned is protector anger? Do you still want to welcome it back? I mentioned earlier that it isn't advisable to encourage clients to express protector anger that is being acted out. However, in the case in which protector anger has been disowned, there are actually two issues to deal with: The first is reowning the anger in order to develop strength, and the second is getting beneath the angry protector to heal the exile it is protecting so the protector can let go.

It is important to reown the anger first—to welcome it back into the internal system and perhaps encourage a client to express it—so that the client can reown his or her strength. Then the client can get to know the protector and get permission to work with and heal its exile, so the angry protector can then let go. This way, the client gets the benefits of both processes. If you work on understanding the anger as protection first, you may lose the possibility of helping the client to regain his or her disowned strength.

Working with Protectors
That Block Healthy Aggression

In the course of welcoming back anger, protectors are often activated that are frightened of the anger or the associated strength and aliveness. Therefore, in the process of welcoming back the anger, you will need to work with these parts.

You must also pay attention to any of your (therapist's) parts that may be uneasy with anger. If you aren't completely comfortable with anger, you may subtly side with the client's protectors, or, at least, you may not fully support and encourage the client's anger when that is what's needed. If necessary, do your own IFS work with your protectors so you can completely support your clients' anger and strength.

When a protector is activated that blocks the client from welcoming back his or her anger, first ask it if it would be willing to step aside so that the healing process can continue. If it won't, ask the protector what it is afraid of, and reassure it about its fears. If necessary, spend a session or more working with the protector to relax these fears.

A protector like this is often afraid that the client will do dangerous things with the anger. In fact, sometimes there is rage that has been suppressed, and protectors are afraid that it will be explosive and destructive if allowed to come out. Often the rage is so explosive **because** it has been suppressed and exiled in the client's psyche. The more the angry part is exiled, the angrier it becomes.

Reassure those protectors that, as you get to know the rageful part, the client will remain in Self with your help, and therefore the rage won't get out of control. You can reassure the protectors that if the rage is expressed at all, it will only be done in therapy sessions, not in the client's life.

A protector may be afraid that the client will be attacked, judged, or ridiculed by others for showing anger. Reassure the protector that **you** welcome the anger and would never judge or ridicule the client for expressing it. (Do your own work on yourself to make sure that this is true.)

The client can also reassure the protector that if the anger is expressed in real life, the client's Self will remain in charge and not allow any destructive acting out. The client will instead express the anger constructively and will choose situations where it is safe to do so.

If the protector won't step aside based on these reassurances, turn your attention to it and give it a full IFS session or series of sessions, which may involve accessing and unburdening the exile being protected by the anger-blocking protector. You can also do a polarization session between the angry part and this protector. (See my book *Resolving Inner Conflict* for how to work with polarization.) This work with the protector will lead to the relaxation of its protective stance, and then you can proceed with integrating the anger and strength into the client's psyche.

For example, when Donna first expressed her anger, a protector came up that was frightened that she would be abandoned by everyone for being angry and strong. It stopped her by making her go blank so she couldn't feel the anger any longer. She reassured this part that she wouldn't express the anger inappropriately and that she (in Self) would be there for her angry part. Then the protector was willing to step aside and allow Donna to embody her anger in a session. If this hadn't worked, we could have done a session with the protector that included witnessing how her parents had withdrawn from her when she was angry and unburdening the exile who experienced this abandonment.

In some cases, it isn't simply a matter of welcoming back the disowned anger because it may be hard to find. There may be parts that block even the experience of anger, so the client can only get in touch with sadness or fear. If you consistently notice that exiles only feel pain and never experience anger about what was done to them, it would be wise to check with the client to see if there is a protector blocking his or her anger. Then you can work with this protector to gain access to the disowned anger.

The Expression of Anger

In many cases, a part will experience anger and express it internally in the client's imagination. This might involve imagining shouting, hitting, shaking someone, or even being violent. In many cases, the client will be happy to engage in this internal expression of anger but show no desire to express it outwardly, even in a session. Outward expression of anger isn't always necessary, but if the client has chronically disowned his or her anger and strength, just expressing it internally, though helpful, is usually not enough. The person must embody his or her aggression and express it outwardly in order to gain full access to his or her strength.

Therefore, you may need to ask the client if such a part would like to express the anger physically, using the client's voice and body. It is fine if he or she says no to this in any given session, but if this happens repeatedly, I would advise you to ask the client if the part doesn't want to express the anger outwardly because there are protectors who won't allow it. This usually uncovers a protector that doesn't think it is safe to show anger or, in some cases, to be strong. You then have a chance to work with the protector to allow the full embodiment and expression of the anger that will foster the client's strength.

It is especially important to work with any parts of **yours** that might be afraid of the full expression of a client's anger. If you have a history of being frightened by a parent's anger or physically abused, the exiles who experienced this will need to be healed so you can be fully open to the expression of your clients' anger.

Let's look at an example. As a child, Diane had made an unspoken pact with her father that if she deferred to him and didn't develop her strength or competence in the world, he would always love and protect her. Diane's father reneged on this pact, and she is now in her fifties and her father has died, but one of her parts has nevertheless kept this pact. As a result, it has been hard for Diane to become powerful and successful in her life, and she has had difficulty asserting herself.

As we explored this in her sessions, the exile that kept this pact expressed anger about it as well as about the father's betrayal quite a few times, but always silently through imagery. When I suggested that she might want to express the anger out loud, Diane said the exile didn't need that. However, after many sessions, I became suspicious. I asked if there were protectors who didn't want her to express this anger outwardly, and she immediately realized that there were.

As we explored this, we uncovered more protectors that prohibited her personal power and that were connected to exiles who were frightened of being strong and successful. As we worked with these protectors, they gradually relaxed and stepped aside, allowing Diane to embody her anger and aggression by feeling powerful in her arms and back, with deeper breathing and fire in her eyes.

The next step was to express the anger through her voice, which involved working with even more protectors who were blocking the outward expression of her aggression and strength. They were protecting deeper exiles who were terrified of abandonment and death. As we unburdened these parts, she was able to fully express her anger in an outward, embodied way. This work has given Diane increased access to her personal power, allowing her to assert herself in ways that have made a substantial difference in her life.

Integrating Anger into One's Life

Once clients have welcomed back their disowned anger in sessions, they must learn how to integrate it into their interactions with people in a healthy way. They often begin to feel unusually angry at people they are relating to. They snap at people, or they feel hostile without expressing it directly, and it leaks out. The anger that has been repressed and disowned all their lives is finally coming out. The Angry Part is not only angry about a certain incident that triggers it—it is also annoyed at having been suppressed for so long and angry at all the ways that the client has pleased and kowtowed to people.

The client hasn't yet figured out how to integrate anger into his or her interactions in a healthy way, so it just comes out in a raw form. Clients often go overboard with their aggression for a while until they can find a healthy way to express it. The pendulum had been too far on the suppression side all their lives, and now it swings too far in the expression direction, until it can finally find its rightful place in the middle.

This can be very disconcerting for clients as well as people they are interacting with. The protectors that originally disowned the anger now feel they were justified. "Look what is happening. See, I told you that anger is a bad thing." A polarization is set up between the angry part and protectors that want to squelch the anger.

It is important for you, the therapist, to recognize that the client's anger must not be discouraged, even when it is extreme. The expression of anger, at this point, is a healthy step in the right direction. You don't want to simply access and heal the exile being protected by the anger and then ask the angry part to let go of its anger. Even though the anger **is** a protector and **is** being extreme, the client is in the process of reowning his or her strength. It is important not to undermine this process.

In fact, part of the reason that the anger is extreme is that the angry part is fighting against the protectors that don't like it and want to suppress it. Be careful not to side with those protectors.

You can help the client to get to know the angry part and appreciate the positive qualities it is bringing to the client's life, even though the anger is currently extreme. You might have to work with the polarization between the angry part and the suppressing protector in order to accomplish this. Once the client, in Self, truly appreciates the angry part, it often relaxes and becomes less extreme. The angry part is now connected to and cooperating with the Self. This gives the client (in Self) the opportunity to provide guidance so that the anger can be expressed in a constructive way in real-life interactions with people.

This supports the conversion of anger to strength. The end result is that the client will be stronger and more assertive, and his or her anger, if it is there at all, will be more appropriate to the situation. The client may need some coaching from you about how to interact with people from strength rather than anger. This includes speaking for parts, as discussed earlier, as well as other ways to be firm and powerful without being reactive.

Let's look at an example. My client Debbie had disowned her anger all her life. Instead she was a pleaser. In childhood, she was abused, both physically and sexually, and had relatively little in the way of positive attachment. The only way she could cope was to try to please her parents. This pleasing continued in her marriage and her friendships.

In our therapy, she not only accessed and healed the exiles who were abused and deprived, she also uncovered her anger at what had been done to her. As she expressed this anger in sessions, she gradually began to feel more and more angry in her life. She identified a part she called her Inner Bitch who wanted to yell at people whenever she felt they weren't respecting her boundaries or her needs.

She felt ambivalent toward the Inner Bitch. While she appreciated it in some ways, she basically felt that it was a serious problem because it threatened to undermine her relationships. In one session, I helped her to get to know the Inner Bitch in detail. It told her that its job was to keep people from overpowering her and not respecting her needs. It would do anything to protect her, and it didn't care about the consequences. It really didn't like the pleasing part of her.

She had protectors that judged the Inner Bitch harshly. I helped her to get them to step aside so she could be in Self as she got to know the Bitch. She came to really appreciate what her Inner Bitch was trying to do for her and the strength it had to offer her.

Once she conveyed to the Bitch her appreciation for it, the part softened. It let go of its extreme angry posture and became quite willing to work with Debbie to express itself through strength rather than rage. The term "Inner Bitch" was a somewhat derogatory name for this part, and once Debbie's relationship with it shifted, she asked the part what it wanted to be called, and it chose "The Bodyguard."

In this session, I didn't try to work with the exiles who were being protected by the Bodyguard. We had already unburdened them a fair amount, and though there is probably more work to be done with them, it was important in this session to just support Debbie in connecting with the Bodyguard. We can work with those exiles in future sessions, and this may help the Bodyguard to be less extreme, if that becomes necessary.

As it turned out, as a result of Debbie's new connection with her Bodyguard, its overblown angry reactions gradually subsided and were replaced by a solid ability to be assertive and set limits.

CHAPTER 3

Exile Anger

Exiles may also hold anger, even if the anger itself isn't disowned. Exiles frequently feel angry at the way they were treated in childhood. For example, Sally's older sister made fun of her whenever she tried to play with the sister and her friends. This caused one of Sally's exiles to feel shame, and, in addition, the exile also felt angry at her sister. Exile anger like this is different from protector anger because it is felt **along with** the shame. If it were protector anger, it would arise to **block** the feeling of shame.

With exile anger, the exile should be encouraged to feel (and possibly express) its anger with the Self as witness. In Sally's case, the exile needed to internally express its anger at the sister. This is part of the witnessing step that needs to happen before any exile is ready to unburden. Witnessing an exile's anger may happen before or after the exile's pain is witnessed. Then the exile can unburden its pain and negative beliefs.

In this situation, you may have to work with protectors that are afraid of expressing the anger through imagination, especially expressing it to a parent who would have had rageful or violent reactions if the client had expressed this anger as a child. Help the client to imagine protecting the exile from the parent's angry reaction so the child part feels safe in expressing itself. Explain to the client that the Self can be as large and strong as is needed to handle even a large father. Have the client imagine that he or she (in Self) is much bigger and stronger than the father is, so the client's Self can easily protect the exile from him and therefore allow it to fully express its anger.

Healthy Aggression and the Corrective Emotional Experience

When the original childhood situation involved harm of some kind, it is helpful if the client has access to healthy aggression during the healing process. During the reparenting[6] step in the IFS process, the exile often wants the Self to protect it from the harm that happened in the past by stopping the parent (or other person) who perpetrated the harm. This act of protection sometimes involves expressing anger at the perpetrator, though it can be done without anger as well. This protection makes the exile feel safe and is therefore good preparation for retrieving the exile and unburdening it. Sometimes the exile even wants to be the one to express the anger, with the support and protection of the Self.

When this act of protection does involve anger, it is more effective and healing if it is done with embodied, expressive, healthy aggression. It provides the client with the experience of feeling protected and safe, and also powerful and strong. This is a corrective emotional experience that redresses the exile's original experience of being weak and powerless, and being harmed or even traumatized. In fact,

---

6. *Reparenting* is a term that I have introduced. Richard Schwartz sees this as a preliminary aspect of retrieval. I see it as a separate step in the IFS process that is important in itself.

for clients who are working on trauma, I believe that expressing anger in this way is an important aspect of the healing process.

You may be wondering why I am using the term *reparenting* in this case. When the Self provides the protection, this is obviously reparenting because the Self is providing a protective function that a good parent should provide. However, even when the exile wants to protect itself by expressing anger, this is possible only because the Self is there supporting the exile to do this and protecting it from any reaction from the parent. So even this is a form of reparenting.

However, the larger issue here is that this is a corrective emotional experience. This is the main function of the reparenting step in the IFS process, whether or not it actually looks like reparenting. I have called it the *reparenting* step simply because the corrective emotional experience takes the form of reparenting a great majority of the time.

Let's look at an example. Walt had an exile that was intensely activated whenever he was judged by his boss at his job. The work with this part went back to a childhood scene in which Walt was physically abused by his mother. The first time he worked on this, I encouraged Walt to enter the scene as Self and see what the exile needed from him. It wanted him to stop the mother from hurting the exile, which he imagined doing. Then the exile went through an unburdening process that seemed to be successful.

However, during the next week, Walt was still upset when he was around his boss. When we worked on this in a second session, Walt's exile was still frightened of his mother. This time he felt a desire to stop the mother in a much more overtly aggressive way. With my encouragement, he stood up, repeatedly yelled at her to stop, and executed a series of karate-like kicks. This gave him an embodied experience of the power of being able to protect the exile, and the result was that the exile felt much safer, and its fear greatly diminished.

This produced a spontaneous unburdening[7] that lasted. Walt was much more at ease with his boss after that. The physical expression of Walt's anger was crucial to his ability to fully unburden the fear. Somatic Experiencing[8] has a similar understanding of the value of healthy aggression in the renegotiation of trauma.

What made this aggression "healthy" is that it was only acted out in therapy sessions, not in real life. The Self was in charge and therefore could choose to act out the aggression when it would be healing and wouldn't hurt anyone. If this anger were acted out in the client's life, it would probably be harmful to others. The healthy way to handle this anger in real life would be to speak **for** the angry part, as discussed earlier.

---

7. A spontaneous unburdening is one that doesn't require the explicit unburdening ritual. It happens naturally through other IFS processes.

8. Peter A. Levine, *Healing Trauma: Restoring the Wisdom of the Body*, Sounds True, 1999.

CHAPTER 4

Example Session:
Transforming Rage into Strength

Dorothy was a participant in one of my classes in which I was teaching about working with anger in IFS. She volunteered to work on a part of her that was angry but had been suppressed.

Jay: OK, Dorothy, whenever you're ready.

Dorothy: I have a sense of not having a right to live, and this has been huge in my life. That message was given to me in so many different ways by totally insensitive parents. Some of my difficulty in taking care of my exiles is because of rage at my parents. There's a part of me that's saying, "No, I shouldn't have to do this. *You're* the one who should have nurtured me." I can't remember how many ways they made it clear to me that I shouldn't have been allowed to live, that I was a mistake. And what drove me crazy was that my parents were so beautiful and real.

J: So the part you want to work with is the part that's enraged at them. Is that right?

D: Absolutely, and yet it's terrifying.

J: OK, so it sounds like there's a part that's enraged at them, and there's some other part of you that's terrified of the rage. Is that right?

D: Yes, that is right.

J: OK, so it sounds like we should start with the part that's terrified of the rage. Does that make sense?

The Terrified Part is a protector that isn't allowing the rage to be felt or expressed. We start with the protector so we can get its permission to work with the Rageful Part.

D: Yes, totally.

J: OK. So go inside and focus on that part. And let me know when you're in touch with it.

D: Well, the part that's terrified, I can feel it in my body. I'm shaking. My knees are shaking.

J: Alright, say hello to that part to let it know that you want to get to know it.

D: My whole body is shaking.

J: Uh huh. So ask that Terrified Part if it would be willing to separate from you a little bit so you can help it.

Since her body is shaking with fear, I am assuming that she's blended with the Terrified Part. So I work on unblending.

D: It's growling.

J: Let it know that we're not asking it to go away—we're just asking it to leave a little room for you to be there so you can be there for it.

I interpret the growling as a refusal to separate, so I attempt to reassure the Terrified Part that separation doesn't mean being dismissed.

> **D:** It says, "I don't trust that."

> **J:** So ask the part what it's afraid would happen if it left you some room to be there.

> **D:** That part is quite hysterical; it's just screaming. It says, "I don't know."

> **J:** Mm hmm. Ask it what it's feeling.

> **D:** It says, "I'm afraid of her. I'm afraid of him. I'm afraid of everybody. I'm afraid of the war. I don't know what's going to happen."

> **J:** Is this the part that's afraid of your Rageful Part?

Since this part seems to be afraid of many things, I am checking to see if we have the right part—the one that is afraid of her rage.

> **D:** Yeah. But it's got everything all mixed up that could possibly punish it.

> **J:** OK. So how are you feeling toward this part right now?

It is the right part, and now she seems to have some separation from it, so I ask how she feels toward it to check to see if she's in Self with respect to it.

> **D:** I'm partially blended with it and partially sort of exasperated with it. So I'm not in Self.

> **J:** OK. So the part that's exasperated with it, does that part want to say a little bit about the exasperation?

D: It says, "You've been doing this too long." It's saying to the other part, "It's about time we got angry at these hypocrites who are so beautiful on the outside."

J: I agree that it would be good to express the anger, but being exasperated with the Rageful Part is not going to help. So see if that part, in the service of getting to the anger, would be willing to step aside so that you can be in Self with this Terrified Part.

D: It's grudgingly saying, "OK, a little bit."

She has identified a concerned part that is exasperated with the Terrified Part. I encourage it to say its piece and then reassure it that if it steps aside, this will lead to expressing the anger, which is what it wants. This seems to work.

J: OK, good. So check and see how you're feeling toward the Terrified Part now.

D: I'm feeling a little relieved, and I'm much more separate from it. I'm still feeling a lot of physical energy moving in my body, but it isn't quite shaking so much—it's sort of like moving … in waves.

J: OK. Sounds good. And how are you feeling toward that part?

D: More tolerant, but not quite enough to be in Self. I'm not really welcoming it.

J: OK. Is it still the Exasperated Part that hasn't really completely moved aside, or is it some other part?

D: It's still the Exasperated Part.

J: See if that part would be willing to step aside a little more in the service of getting to the anger.

The Exasperated Part hadn't completely stepped aside, so I ask it again.

D: Something very strange is happening energetically— like energy moving way inside my body.

J: What kind of energy?

D: It's angry energy ...

J: Check and see if the Terrified Part is still there.

D: It's OK. The Terrified Part stood aside.

J: So I'm guessing that its standing aside has led to this angry energy that you're feeling.

Not only has the concerned part (Exasperated Part) stepped aside, but the Terrified Part has as well. So now she has access to the Rageful Part.

D: It seems so ... There's a Rageful Part that's like jumping up and down, and it's kind of celebrating that the energy has come forth. It's a deep black. And now it's shooting sparks on a primitive level.

J: And how are you feeling toward it?

D: Surprised. A little bit curious. A very wee bit frightened, but not seriously.

J: Good. So just encourage that part to express itself, to let you know about itself in any way it wants.

She seems to be in Self now, so I encourage the part to express itself.

D: It says, "I'm the pure energy of rage." It's doing like a war dance … Oh wow, I suddenly got something. A therapist once said to me, "I bet you felt responsible for the whole of World War II." And here it is. If World War II hadn't already happened, I would have waged it.

J: That much rage, huh?

D: Oh, yes. It wants to kill my parents and almost everybody I knew growing up. Not too mercifully, either.

J: OK. So just invite that part to do whatever it wants to do.

D: Whoa! My whole body is shaking again. Really shaking, like, my arms are shaking—big, big gestures. Whoa!

J: Good. Let that happen.

Even though this Rageful Part is probably a protector, I am treating it primarily as a disowned part. In other words, because her anger has been suppressed, I think it is more important for her to feel it and express it in order to develop strength than to get beneath it to the exile it might be protecting. That can come later.

D: Whoa. Yeah, now it's really saying angry things. It's saying, "I hate you. I hate you."

J: Yeah. Just invite that part to use your body and your voice as much as it wants to, to express itself.

I am encouraging her to express the anger physically as a way of more fully embodying the rage and therefore the strength.

D: "I hate you, I hate you." Grrrr ... argh. Argh ... Grraah. [continued shouting, growling noises] Yeah, it doesn't want to talk language.

J: Yeah, that's fine.

D: Whoa!

J: What's happening?

D: It's shaking my body a lot—convulsively. Suddenly and convulsively shaking my body. [more shouting, growling noises]

Now the energy has shifted. Now it's a kind of invigorating energy. Now it doesn't have anger—it's just energy. It's amazing! Yeah. Because it's going up my spine and into my hands.

The anger has turned into pure strength.

J: So let's treat that energy as a part and just say hello to that energy, that part. See what it has to say.

D: It's amazing because now it's going into my head. It's really in my whole body. And it's not like anything I've ever experienced.

J: So ask it what it does for you.

D: It says, "I've been trapped all this time. I am your right to exist. And I've been waiting to move through you. I've been waiting to inhabit you."

This makes it clear that this is indeed a disowned part, so we welcome it back into her internal family.

J: Well, welcome it in!

D: Wow! I'm beginning to feel just the beginning of tears. Because in some of the work that I did recently, I really was aware that before I was born, someone wanted to get rid of me. And that fetus or embryo knew. So it's a long time coming—this energy.

J: So the tears come from your being moved?

D: Yeah.

J: How do you feel that energy in your body now—that right-to-live energy?

D: It's very physical. It's a good thing you asked me that. Because I can feel it in my fingers. I can feel it in my back. But it's not enough in my lungs. This past week I've had a respiratory infection, and when I was a baby I almost died of one. So there's this battle going on. This battle for life is being reenacted. I don't feel the energy going all the way into my feet. So like my lungs and my feet are not letting it in, and yet I can feel it in my voice. I'm speaking a little more loudly.

J: Just take some time to really enjoy feeling that energy in all the parts of your body where it is. Really let yourself inhabit that—feel it, and enjoy it.

D: Whoa. It's really powerful! But there's this huge contrast between the whole rest of my body and my lungs and my feet, which aren't letting it in.

Notice how much she is embodying the right-to-live energy, which is strength. This will help her to be more fully vibrant.

D: Now I can see an animal. It's a panther or something. And it's growling. [more growling noises]

The part has switched back to angry energy, so I ask about the focus of the anger.

J: Is it growling at anybody in particular? Does it want to growl at your parents or your family, or just do it in general?

D: It's saying, "Don't mess with me. You're idiots. Don't tell me about how I'm not supposed to be *me*. If you don't like me, it's *your* problem." [laughter]

There are two healing processes going on here as well as other points in this session. One is that Dorothy is reowning her anger and developing strength. The other is that she is reworking an old childhood situation. Originally she was made to feel bad about herself and as though she didn't deserve to live. Part of the healing process with an exile is to provide it with an emotional experience that is a corrective to that original situation. In this case, the Self is supporting the exile to fight back against the original harm. The exile is declaring its sense of value and right to exist, and it is protecting itself from the experience of feeling that its life is threatened.

Richard Schwartz sees this corrective activity as a preliminary aspect of retrieval. I see it as a separate step in the IFS process that is important in itself. In Self-Therapy, *I call this the "reparenting" step because, almost all the time, it involves the Self reparenting the exile, but it can involve any kind of corrective emotional experience.*

D: It's amazing that that came out of me. That's something new! [more laughter] I don't believe that came out of me! Wow!

J: Joy coming up, huh?

She is responding to her anger and reworking the childhood situation with excitement, and her laughter has a joyous quality to it. She seems to be celebrating her strength.

D: Oh, yeah. I like that. "If you don't like me, it's *your* problem." Oh wow! There are a lot of people I want to say that to from my childhood, and adolescence, and young adulthood, including my family—my scapegoating family.

J: So what are you feeling now?

D: I'm feeling relief. I'm still not quite breathing deeply enough in my lungs. I'm getting more grounded in my feet. I'm feeling my toes more. And my eyes are releasing a little. So it's just the lungs that haven't caught up yet. [pause]

Yeah, I don't know why I'm not breathing deeply enough, but the rest of me feels amazing. You know, it's just what you said, Jay, about regaining strength. I mean, the rest of me is feeling strong, in a way that's quite unfamiliar. I'm not used to this. This is extraordinary—quite alien to me.

I had taught the class about the relationship between anger and strength. Notice that the more she expresses her anger, the more fully the energy inhabits her body.

D: The other thing I notice is that I'm not free in my shoulders.

J: So check now to see if you're aware of any parts that are blocking either the lungs or the movement in your shoulders.

Since the energy is still blocked from parts of her body, I ask about the parts that might be blocking it.

D: It feels like there's a part that's too young to speak. Oh wow! You know what it feels like? It feels like a part that's afraid of being born—that's afraid to come out of the womb.

J: All right. Let's focus on that part. How are you feeling toward that part?

D: I'm somewhat blended with it, but not too much. I feel concerned for it.

J: So just ask the part to let you know, in some way, more about its fear of being born.

D: Yeah. It says, "I'm afraid to stay inside, and I'm afraid to come out."

J: Ask it what it's afraid of about coming out.

D: It says, "They're going to let me die. And it will be no good if I live, either."

J: Ask it what it's afraid of about living.

D: It just says, "It's going to be horrible. She already hates me."

J: And that makes this part really scared, huh?

D: Yup, terrified. Shaking, energetic shaking.

She has contacted an exile that's holding fear about being born. You may notice that here, and in other places in this session, she has parts that are very young and seem to have information that only older parts should have, such as the fact that her mother will hate her. I think that young parts often have access to information that comes from older parts without necessarily realizing that this is happening.

J: Just see if there's anything else that this part wants you to know about what this was like.

D: It's no good in there, either. See, I was born one month premature. And they didn't expect to save both of us. Ooh, you know what? Wow! I think this little being knew something that my parents told me. I was about seven when they told me this: My mother almost died when I was born, and they asked my father which one they should save. And he said, "Of course, save the mother. I can always have another child."

What I'm getting now is that, in some sense, this part knew. It knew that it wasn't supposed to live. And there's a part of me that would have wanted to kill her … let *her* die. Yeah, there's a part of me that's saying, "Let *her* die. Let *me* live, and let *her* die." How about *that?*

J: So that's some more anger.

The exile's fear has shifted to rage.

D: Rage—murderous rage. Ooh, you know what? I'm able to get more air. Wow! I'm able to breathe quite a bit better.

As she expresses more of the rage, her energy is able to gradually fill out her body completely.

D: And there's another rage that I'm getting in touch with, from another exile. It's an older exile that was seven or eight years old when both parents told her the entire story, from before conception, about how terrible it was for them.

J: So that's the part that's enraged about them telling a young child that story?

D: Yes, because it was terrifying. They told me the whole thing. I'm not going to go into the whole of it now. I mean, it was terrible for them, but to tell me about it when I was seven-and-a-half ...

J: Yeah, so just encourage that part's rage.

D: Yeah, that part just wants to scream and scream. It's saying, "You *don't* know who I am. You *never* knew who I was. You lived and died without knowing who I am. Both of you!"

Yeah, it was totally terrifying, the story they told me—about her pregnancy, and what they went through, and what they did.

J: So this part's letting you know how terrifying that was.

D: Terrifying—totally terrifying. It's a whole drama. I mean it really happened, but to tell that to a kid who isn't even eight years old ... And then when she was pregnant with my sister, I was petrified that she would die.

J: So, the last part you were in touch with, with the rage, has that part gotten it out? Has that part expressed it? Does it need to say more or show you more?

D: My body is shaking again, a lot.

J: Shaking with fear or rage?

D: No, no. It's just shaking with energy.

This shaking is probably the expression of the fear. The fear is being experienced and expressed without being blocked and without it blocking her experience of anger and strength. I think the shaking is also a release or spontaneous unburdening of the fear.

J: All right. Just let that happen.

D: Yeah. It's like wildly shaking my knees and my arms. And actually, now it's shaking my whole body. Yeah, wow! Ooh. And the Panther is showing up again. It seems like it is happy about what we're doing. And I'm identifying with being a cat, the teeth and the claws. [pause]

J: What needs to happen next?

It seems that she has now felt and expressed the rage and embodied strength as much as she needs to, at least for this session. So now she switches her attention to one of the exiles that she accessed.

D: I just want to see if I can find that exile and check in with it.

J: Which—the seven-year-old or the one before birth?

D: The one being born.

J: OK, good. So check in with that.

D: It wants me to bring her into *my* belly. And it wants me to keep remembering that she's in there, so she's able to feel herself.

She is now reparenting this exile.

> **J:** So she's going to be *your* baby, huh?

> **D:** Yeah. She wants to be *my* baby. And she wants to stay there as long as she wants to, until we do more work with her so that she's ready to be born. So I'm taking her into myself. And I'm asking her if she's OK now, and she says yes.

> **J:** Good. That's perfect. You can let her stay there as long as she needs and work with her more, until she's ready ... So let's stop there.

There is more work to do with this exile who was afraid to be born, but this is enough for one session.

> **D:** Thank you. Incredible.

This session demonstrates beautifully how reowning one's anger and rage leads to strength and vibrancy as well as increased self-esteem and joy. It also shows how the expression of anger can be a corrective emotional experience

CHAPTER 5

Conclusion

Expressing Anger in Therapy

There have been many discussions in the psychotherapy field about the value of expressing anger in psychotherapy sessions and potential problems with this. Therapists writing about this issue have tended to take black-and-white positions. It either **is** or **isn't** a good idea to encourage clients to express anger. As you can see from this booklet, this is not a simple question. Sometimes outward expression of anger is valuable, and sometimes it is dangerous.

The distinctions made in this booklet can help us to understand when it is advisable to encourage the outward expression of anger and when it is not, how to express the anger, and what purpose this expression might serve. Let's look at the possibilities:

1. Protector anger serves a defensive purpose. It needs to be understood, but usually expressing it will only strengthen the defense. This is especially true with anger that is being acted out in the world; expressing it might encourage more acting out. A client with protector anger can benefit from practicing how to communicate it in a constructive way.

2. Exile anger needs to be witnessed. It may be expressed outwardly or not, depending on what the exile wants.

In some cases, expressing anger can provide a corrective emotional experience as part of the healing process.

3. Disowned anger usually needs to be expressed in sessions as a way of accessing and developing the client's strength and healthy aggression. This expression should be as full and embodied as possible.

Help Sheet

The following is an outline of the various circumstances and dynamics around anger that have been presented in this booklet and a summary of the steps to deal with each one.

A. Protector Anger Acted Out

1. Get to know the angry protector.
2. Help the client learn to contain the anger in life situations.
3. Teach the client how to speak **for** the angry part rather than **from** it.
4. Get permission to work with the exile that the angry part is protecting.
5. Go through the steps to help and unburden that exile.
6. Help the angry protector to let go of its angry role.

B. Protector Rage Felt but Suppressed, or Protector Rage Repressed with Occasional Outbursts

1. Work with the polarization between the enraged part and the blocking protector.
2. Get permission to get to know the enraged part.
3. Heal its exile so the protector can let go, as in A4–A6.

C. Disowned Anger

1. Work with disowning protectors to get their permission to work with the angry part.
2. Welcome the angry part into the client's inner family.
3. Encourage expression of the anger in sessions in order to develop strength.
4. Work with protectors that judge the expression of anger in the client's life.
5. Encourage the client to appreciate what the angry part has to offer and develop a trusting relationship with it.
6. Help the client to integrate the anger into his or her interactions with people as strength.

D. Protector Anger Disowned

1. Welcome the angry part in order to gain access to the client's strength, as in C.
2. Later, in separate sessions, deal with it in the regular IFS way, as in A4–A6.

E. Exile Anger

1. Witness the anger just as with any other exile emotion.
2. Help the client to express the anger outwardly if the exile wants to do so.
3. Work with any protectors that are preventing the anger from being expressed outwardly.
4. Encourage the expression of anger toward a parent during the reparenting step as a corrective emotional experience, if the exile wants that.

Summary

This booklet contains a detailed exploration of various ways to work with anger in IFS. It shows that anger comes up in a variety of contexts and needs to be handled differently in each one. In some cases, it needs to be witnessed and healed in the regular IFS way. In other situations, the client needs to learn to contain it and communicate it constructively. In still others, the client needs to feel and express it fully in a session as a way of developing strength. And sometimes anger is an aid in the healing process. In many cases, protectors that block the anger must be worked with, sometimes including work on the polarization between the protector and the angry part.

Appendix A

Glossary

Blending. A situation in which a part has taken over a client's consciousness so that the client feels its feelings, believes its attitudes are true, and acts according to its impulses.

Burden. A painful emotion or negative belief about oneself or the world that a part has taken on as a result of a past harmful situation or relationship, usually from childhood.

Concerned Part* A part that feels judgmental or angry toward the protector you are focusing on. When a client is blended with a concerned part, he or she isn't in Self. Richard Schwartz sees this as a manager that is polarized with the protector.

Disowned Part* A part that has been exiled because it was unacceptable in the client's family of origin. When the disowned part is a protector, Richard Schwartz calls it a protector-in-exile.

Exile. A part that is carrying pain from the past, usually a young child part. It has been pushed into the unconscious and exiled from the client's internal family.

Firefighter. A type of protector that impulsively jumps in when the pain of an exile is starting to surface in order to distract the client from the pain or numb it.

---

* This is a term that I introduced that is not part of the official IFS terminology.

Manager. A type of protector that proactively tries to arrange a client's life and psyche so that an exile's pain isn't felt.

Part. A subpersonality, which has its own feelings, perceptions, beliefs, motivations, and memories.

Polarization. A situation in which two parts are in conflict about how a client should act or feel.

Protector. A part that tries to block off pain that is arising inside or to protect a client from hurtful incidents or distressing relationships in his or her current life. A manager or firefighter.

Protector-in-Exile. A protector that has been exiled because it was unacceptable in the client's family of origin.

Reparenting* The step in the IFS process in which the Self gives an exile a corrective emotional experience with respect to a harmful childhood situation. Richard Schwartz sees this as a preliminary part of the retrieval process.

Retrieval. The step in the IFS process in which the Self takes an exile out of a harmful childhood situation and into a place where it can be safe and comfortable.

Self. The core aspect of a person that is his or her true self or spiritual center. The Self is relaxed, open, and accepting of oneself and others. It is curious, compassionate, calm, and interested in connecting with other people and the person's parts.

Self-Leadership. A situation in which a client's parts trust the client, in Self, to make decisions and take action in his or her life.

Speaking For a Part. A person is in Self, describing the feelings of a part, not acting it out.

Speaking From a Part. A person is blended with the part and is acting out its feelings.

Spontaneous Unburdening. An unburdening that doesn't require the explicit unburdening ritual because it happens naturally through other IFS processes.

Strength* Healthy aggression, personal power, forcefulness, limit setting, aliveness, expansiveness, and passion.

Unblending. A client separates from a part that is blended with him or her in order to be in Self.

Unburdening. The step in the IFS process in which the Self helps an exile to release its burdens through an internal ritual.

Witnessing. The step in the IFS process in which the Self witnesses the childhood origin of a part's burdens.

IFS Resources

IFS Therapists

If you want to find an IFS therapist to work with, consult the website of the Center for Self Leadership, the official IFS organization, at www.selfleadership.org. It contains a listing of therapists who have completed Level 1 of the IFS professional training and can be searched by geographical location. Some of these therapists offer IFS sessions by telephone.

IFS Professional Training and Consultation

The Center for Self Leadership conducts IFS training programs, which I highly recommend, for therapists and others in the helping professions. There are three levels, which can be taken one at a time. Level 1 usually consists of six three-day weekends and is also occasionally offered as a retreat-style training with two week-long sessions. These training programs are held in many cities in the U.S. and in Europe. The leaders are excellent, and the curriculum is well designed. These are experiential trainings, so you learn about IFS by working with your own parts and practicing doing sessions with others in the training. There is an emphasis on building community in the training group, which fosters personal and professional connection. See the CSL website, www.selfleadership.org, for details about training locations and schedules.

I lead IFS consultation groups over the telephone, and

I offer a variety of training courses and workshops, many by telephone. See my IFS website www.personal-growth-programs.com for a complete list of offerings.

IFS Classes and Groups

I teach classes for the general public in which people learn to use IFS for self-help and peer counseling. They can be taken by telephone or in person in the San Francisco Bay Area. Each class is either a six-week course or a weekend workshop. Some of the classes are taught by my wife, Bonnie Weiss, and other highly skilled IFS therapists and teachers. Some of these classes will be available as downloadable recordings. We also offer IFS classes and workshops on polarization, procrastination, eating issues, intimacy, communication, and other topics.

I also offer ongoing IFS therapy groups in person as well as ongoing IFS classes over the telephone. See www.personal-growth-programs.com for more information and a schedule of classes and groups.

IFS Books

Introduction to the Internal Family System Model, by Richard Schwartz. A basic introduction to parts and IFS for clients and potential clients.

Internal Family Systems Therapy, by Richard Schwartz. The primary professional book on IFS and a must-read for therapists.

The Mosaic Mind, by Richard Schwartz and Regina Goulding. A professional book on using IFS with trauma, especially sexual abuse.

You Are the One You've Been Waiting For, by Richard Schwartz. A popular book providing an IFS perspective on intimate relationships.

Self-Therapy: A Step-by-Step Guide to Creating Wholeness and Healing Your Inner Child Using IFS, by Jay Earley. Shows how to do IFS sessions on your own or with a partner. Also a manual of the IFS method that can be used by therapists.

Self-Therapy for Your Inner Critic, by Jay Earley and Bonnie Weiss. Shows how to use IFS to work with inner critic parts.

Resolving Inner Conflict, by Jay Earley. Shows how to work through polarization using IFS.

Illustrated Workbook for Self-Therapy for Your Inner Critic, by Bonnie Weiss. A graphic support containing illustrations from the book in large format and grouped for easy understanding.

Parts Work, by Tom Holmes. A short, richly illustrated introduction to IFS for the general public.

Bring Yourself to Love, by Mona Barbera. A book for the general public on using IFS to work through difficulties in love relationships.

IFS Articles and Recordings

The Center for Self Leadership website, www.selfleadership.org, contains professional articles by Richard Schwartz on IFS. He has produced a number of excellent videos of IFS sessions he has conducted that can be purchased from the website. There are also audio recordings of presentations from past IFS conferences.

Bonnie Weiss and I have downloadable recordings of IFS demonstration sessions to help people learn the IFS process. We also have recordings of our IFS classes for the general public for purchase. See our website www.personal-growth-programs.com for details.

IFS Conferences and Workshops

The annual IFS conference is an excellent opportunity to delve more deeply into the Model and network with other professionals. Richard Schwartz leads week-long personal growth workshops open to the public at various growth centers in the U.S. and Mexico. Other professional workshops and presentations on IFS by Schwartz and other top IFS trainers are also offered. See www.selfleadership.org for details.

My Websites and Applications

My IFS website, www.personal-growth-programs.com, contains popular and professional articles on IFS and its application to various psychological issues, and more are being added all the time. You can also sign up for the email list to receive future articles and notification of upcoming classes and groups.

My personal website, www.jayearley.com, contains more of my writings and information about my practice, including my therapy groups.

Another website, www.psychemaps.com, contains a free Inner Critic Questionnaire and Profiling Program for understanding your Inner Critic and developing an Inner Champion to deal with it.

I am developing a web application for doing self-therapy online using IFS. It should be available by the fall of 2012.

Made in the USA
Columbia, SC
20 October 2021

47466024R10046